From Original Artwork to Reproduction: Rights to Ownership
4

Limited Editions: Reproducing Fine Art
6

Common Forms of Printing Limited Editions
8

Certificate Of Authenticity
12

Paper: What You Need To Know
13

Caring For Artwork On Paper
15

Matting and Framing
17

Insuring Art
19

Interesting Laws That Pertain to Art
21

Glossary
22

Published by
MAKE IT SIMPLE PUBLICATIONS

Copyright © 1991 by Doug Thompson

All rights reserved. No part of this book may be reproduced or utilized in any form or by any means, electronic or mechanical, including photocopying, recording, or by any information storage and retrieval system, without permission in writing from the Publisher.

Inquires should be addressed to: Make It Simple Publications, 23052 Alicia Pkwy., Suite H411, Mission Viejo, CA 92692.

ISBN 0-9630775-0-3

Printed in the United States of America.

QUANTITY SALES
This booklet is available at special quantity discounts when purchased in bulk by corporations, organizations and special interest groups. Custom imprinting or excerpting can also be done to fit special needs. For details write: Make It Simple Publications, 23052 Alicia Pkwy., Suite H411, Mission Viejo, CA 92692.

The Survival Guide to Buying Art

PREFACE

What is a serigraph, a lithograph or an etching, and how do they differ? What do the terms "artist proof" and "dedicated proof" mean, and how many of each is the artist allowed to reproduce? How do you prove the authenticity of a piece?

The intention of this book is to simplify what appears to be a rather complex world of terms and reproductive techniques. Its extensive glossary will answer these questions and more, teaching you about everything from paper to art insurance.

With the introduction of new printing technology, art has taken on many and varied forms. The range has expanded from original art, such as paint to canvas or chisel to stone, to a wide range of reproductive options. Each technique has its own unique appeal and function.

This guide will assist you in clarifying elements that have a distinct affect on your art purchase. It also covers many of the legal factors involved in acquiring art, including laws specific to California that many art observers believe will soon apply nationally.

Whether you're a serious collector or first-time buyer, this concise reference will prove to be a convenient "survival guide" to the world of art.

The Survival Guide to Buying Art

FROM ORIGINAL ARTWORK TO REPRODUCTION
Rights to Ownership

Today's artists have many wonderful options to choose from for reproducing an original piece. They can create a mold and cast an original sculpture in a myriad of different materials, from plastic to bronze. They can develop print after print of an original painting, utilizing anything from a high-tech printing process to the intricate technique of hand-pulling paper through a press.

Reproducing an original introduces new issues of ownership. Who owns the original artwork? Who owns the mold? Who owns the image of the painting? To help answer these questions, we'll break down a painting into its component parts.

An original painting has a canvas, paint, frame, stretcher bar and so on. These are known as the "body." If you then take a photograph of that painting, you have created an "image" of the piece. You didn't reproduce it but created something totally different, an "image" with no physical properties common to the original.

The artist (or their representative) may sell you the original art piece or "body," but will retain all rights to the "image" of that same piece. The artist can create reproductions from that image and has indefinite ownership of any photos, molds, plates, etc., that stem from that reproduction.

Because of the new reproductive technology, the image of an original artwork can have considerable long-term value.

Original Art to Reproduction

When purchasing a piece, it's a good idea to ask if the artist has any plans to reproduce its image. If so, the value of your original art will likely increase.

You also can approach the artist (or the agent) to inquire about "backing" the reproduction of a certain piece through a variety of financial options. The artist owns all rights and can make agreements accordingly.

Copyright— Under the U.S. copyright law of January 1, 1978, a copyright is protected on a piece of original art when it becomes "fixed in a tangible form of expression." As soon as the piece is finished, it becomes the property of the artist, for the length of his or her life plus 50 years, and is automatically protected under copyright. Works that were created before the new law came into effect but which had neither been published nor registered before January 1, 1978, are protected by this law. Most artists will place a copyright notice in a location where, if looked for, it can easily be found.

LIMITED EDITIONS
Reproducing Fine Art

When fine art is to be reproduced, the artist must limit the edition of the piece to a predetermined quantity if the work is to retain its integrity and value.

When dealing specifically with an edition of prints, each piece bears two numbers: the first represents its place in the reproductive sequence, and the second is the total number of prints in that edition. If the artist decides the edition total will be 150 and you buy the 8th one produced, the number on it will read 8/150.

Most collectors invest in artwork bearing the lowest available number in the edition, because the higher numbers (or later reproductions) may not be as sharp due to plate wear. When the most modern methods of printing are being used, though, such as offset photolithography, the quality of number 1 and number 500 will be virtually the same. For collection purposes, however, the lowest numbered print available is still the most desirable.

Limited editions will also have the title of the piece and the artist's signature displayed, most commonly in pencil. This information will usually be at the bottom of the print and read: NUMBER - TITLE - ARTIST'S SIGNATURE.

The artist will customarily keep the first proofs from the edition for his or her own copyright use and/or sale. They will be marked "A/P" or "Artist Proof" and bear no number. These prints may also be called "Epreuve D Artiste", or "E/A." Artist proofs usually comprise no more than

Limited Editions

10% of the total edition and may have additional value because they are first off the plate.

Some copies known as "dedicated prints" or "presentation prints," may also be retained by the artist. These are generally not sold but are dedicated to a specific individual or organization. The total number of prints in one edition, in fine art at least, generally stays in the hundreds.

Once the set number has been reproduced, the artist will then either destroy, or deface, the plate used for the reproductions to ensure the integrity of the edition.

COMMON FORMS OF PRINTING LIMITED EDITIONS

Numerous methods are used to reproduce art, and new technology is being introduced every year. The most traditional methods are described here and illustrate why the lower numbers in any edition are the most sought after. Each time a print is pulled or pressed, the plate (or block, etc.) is worn and dulled. Therefore, the lower numbers of the first-run prints are thought to have the sharpest images while the later versions may show a loss in detail. Most artists will only run a small edition in order to ensure that the last print is just as acceptable as the first.

With so many limited-edition prints being offered, some artists will "remarque" their prints for added artistic value. This involves adding a small original drawing or painting to the limited-edition print, usually just outside the printed image area. The artist will normally ask an additional fee for this work, because he or she has created original art on your print, enhancing its value.

ETCHING: A sheet of copper or zinc, used to form the plate, is first coated with an acid-resistant covering called "the ground." The artist then draws the image with etching tools, careful to imprint the ground and expose the metal without scratching the plate. Wherever lines appear on the ground, there will be lines on the final print. The plate is then placed in a solution of diluted acid, which eats into the exposed metal and "etches" grooves into the plate's surface. When the artist is satisfied with the depth of the grooves, the plate is taken from the acid and the remaining ground is removed. Heavy ink is rubbed into the etched grooves using a dauber or lint-free cloth (tarlatan). The artist then wipes the surface of the plate clean, leaving the ink in the grooves. A sheet of damp paper is placed on the inked side of the plate, and both are run through a press. The pressure from the rollers forces the porous paper into the inked grooves, printing the image in reverse and embossing the paper in the process.

LITHOGRAPHY: In the modern world of art, there are at least two different printing methods referred to as lithography. The more traditional process simply called lithography, operates on the principle that oil and water don't mix. An image is drawn with greasy crayons on a surface such as stone, paper or treated aluminum. The printmaker then treats this surface with a special solution and wets it with water, which is absorbed into all areas except the greasy image. When oil-based ink is rolled across the surface, it's repelled by the water and attracted only to the grease-based drawing. A sheet of paper is placed on the treated surface and pressure is applied to the back of the paper (by a mechanical press or a number of hand devices). The image is printed in reverse.

OFFSET PHOTO-LITHOGRAPHY: This modern approach to lithography has revolutionized the print market. The artwork is first photographed, then separated into color negatives that are used to make printing plates. Once

Common Forms of Printing Limited Editions

on the press, the ink is transferred (the offset) from each printing plate to a rubber blanket and onto paper. Numerous colors can be printed at once and at high speed. The printed image is positive.

SERIGRAPHY: This general term for silkscreening is typically used when referring to fine art. A screen of finely woven material, such as silk, is stretched taut on a frame. The artist can paint the design directly on the screen or place on top of it a stencil cut to the desired shape. Areas in the design meant to receive color are left unpainted or open, allowing ink to pass through. A sheet of paper or other suitable material (the final canvas) is placed under the frame. When the ink or paint is wiped across the surface of the screen with a squeegee, it penetrates to the surface below and imprints on the final canvas. By making additional screens for the same design and applying color upon color, the artist can build intricate prints and simulate original paintings. This direct method results in a positive image.

RELIEF: Wood, rubber, plastic, linoleum and other materials are all used as plates for this type of printing. The artist uses sharp tools to cut away areas he or she does not want to print, leaving the desired design to be printed standing out from the background. Dense, sticky ink is rolled onto this raised surface of the plate. A sheet of paper is then placed on the inked plate and rubbed to transfer the image (a press is sometimes used). The paper is then gently pulled away from the plate, leaving the image printed in reverse.

Common Forms of Printing Limited Editions

MONOPRINT: This technique combines painting and printing. The image is drawn, using oil-based or water-based mediums, onto a flat plate consisting of metal, glass, wood, plastic or other material. Damp paper (most commonly) is laid directly on the plate and rubbed or pressed. When the paper is lifted, the image is revealed in reverse. This is a one-time process.

COLLAGRAPH: The plate for this process consists of bits of paper, fabric or other material that have been combined and affixed to a surface. Usually sealing the plate with a medium beforehand, the artist works printing ink into the texture of the plate where it collects in the edges and grooves of the design. The smoother the area, the lighter the tones. After wiping the excess ink away, the artist places damp paper on the surface of the plate and prints, usually with an etching press. The resulting image is embossed and appears in reverse.

INTAGLIO: In this process—which is used with mezzotint, engraving, drypoint, etching and aquatint—images are cut below the surface of the plate. As in the etching process, ink is forced into the grooves, then the surface is wiped clean. With a press, the dampened paper is forced into the grooves to pick up the ink which prints the image in reverse. Intaglio is distinguished from other methods of printing because the finished image appears embossed and the print normally bears a platemark.

CERTIFICATE OF AUTHENTICITY

Artists use a certificate of authenticity to guarantee their limited editions. Such certificates are valuable and should be requested by the art buyer when not offered, at the time of purchase.

In reference to fine art prints, the certificate should include: the title of the piece, artist's name and/or studio, total number of prints, sequence number of the print, and type of paper on which the edition was printed. A statement guaranteeing that no prior edition exists and that none will be printed in the future should also appear on the certificate.

Example of Certificate

Certificate of Authenticity

Title _____
Number _____

This certifies that this print by George Sumner has been limited to_____ plus_____artist's proofs signed and numbered reproductions of the original oil painting.

Each reproduction has been printed on acid-free, Ph neutral, Museum quality, 100 lb. paper and personally inspected for quality and accuracy by the artist, verified by his signature.

No prior edition exhists, and no future edition shall be published as the plates have been destroyed by the printer.

George Sumner
AKA, SUMNER FINE ARTS, INC.
Sausalito, California

PAPER
What You Need To Know

Paper is by far the most popular material used for art reproductions, whether they be posters or fine art serigraphs.

Produced in thin sheets, paper can be made from a wide range of fibrous materials including the pulp of rags, straw, bark and wood. The first of its kind, developed in China around 105 B.C., consisted of vegetable fibers that were macerated (torn apart and soaked in liquid), floated in water, collected on a screen and then dried.

Today's process for making paper, by hand or machine, varies little from this original technique. The raw material is literally beaten to a pulp, then left to swell and separate in a water solution. With the use of a sieve-like screen, it's lifted out in the form of a thin layer, then dried. When removed from the screen's surface, the sheet of matted, intertwined fiber carries the texture and color of the raw materials from which it was made. Some of the best paper is made of pure linen rag.

Making paper by hand offers considerable flexibility. Unusual raw materials, even small flowers or petals, can be combined to create a desired effect. Once the pulp is screened, as just described, the papermaker can also personalize the thickness of each piece by adjusting the blank frame (or "deckle") between the screens. When this deckle is removed, the paper has a ragged-edge and is referred to in the industry as "deckled handmade paper."

Paper

A distinctive characteristic of machine-made paper is the identical quality of each sheet. Some machines, however, can now duplicate the handmade deckled edge.

Different artist techniques require different papers. China clay is often added to some papers to smooth out the surface. "HP" (or hot-pressed papers) are the smoothest, having been run through metal cylinders that compress and polish (while adding the clay). Paper produced naturally or treated with felts is often called "rough" while medium textures are known as "cold pressed" (or "Not").

Most paper for art use has been treated to reduce absorbency. It has also been tested for consistency of acidity, evenness, weight, width and strength. When this has been done, the paper is "sized." For best results, all artwork should be on acid-free, pH-neutral, museum-quality paper.

With pesticides and other toxic substances so prevalent in today's organic materials, artists and consumers need to be concerned about the accelerated aging and deterioration that may result.

Watermarks

Watermarks, or insignias, seemed to have begun somewhere around 1300 A.D. A watermark is a translucent design, visible when you hold the paper up to the light. In handmade paper, thin wires (in the shape of the mark) are attached to the surface of the paper mold. This displaces the fibers and thins the sheet over the mark. In machine-made paper, the insignia may be stamped or chemically implanted.

CARING FOR ARTWORK ON PAPER

Some works of art on paper are 2000 years old. Although one of the most vulnerable of mediums, fine art paper should last hundreds of years with proper care.

Climate and Lighting

Artwork on paper is very sensitive to any type of intense light. Paper should not be exposed to the heat of incandescent bulbs, direct or strong sunlight, or unfiltered fluorescent lamps. The ultraviolet rays eminating from fluorescent tubes and sunlight can cause yellowing or bleaching, possibly changing colors in the artwork. Heat can cause paper to dry out and become brittle.

Paper is also affected by environmental elements. Changes in atmospheric pressure create movement of airborne pollutants in the form of minuet water vapors. When combined with the effects of fluctuating temperature and humidity, the impact can be noticeable. It's also wise to keep artwork away from heaters, air conditioners, doors, windows and other dirt sources.

If you see light gray "fuzz" appearing on artwork that's mounted under glass, it could be mold. The spores grow in conditions of moisture, warmth and still air. They will strike certain inks, the glues, starches, and gum bindings in paint, as well as other ingredients that make up artwork.

If this seems to be the case, call a professional organization (such as your local art museum) and ask where you can have the artwork fumigated. This is done in an airtight chamber by professionals only. Avoid using household products of any kind.

Caring for Artwork on Paper

Handling Artwork

When you handle art, wear a pair of inexpensive cotton gloves. Our skin contains acids that can cause deterioration in paper.

An unmounted print (or any artwork on paper) should not be lifted by the corners. Slide a sheet of ragboard under the artwork and lift it by holding the support piece. Never stack different works against one another. When lesser papers, containing contaminating elements, come into contact with higher grade papers, deterioration may begin. Never use paper clips or staples on any artwork.

If you have unframed artwork (matted or not) that needs to be stored, be sure to encase it in 100% acid-free rag board. If possible, place it in drawers such as those built specifically for maps and blueprints.

If your art must be shipped, be sure it can "breathe." Avoid using plastic bags made of polyvinyl chloride, which is potentially harmful to all art. Condensation is a problem with any plastic. Protect your art with tissue paper or some type of layer between it and the wrapping material.

MATTING AND FRAMING

Matting and framing not only enhance your artwork, but protect it as well. Therefore it's highly suggested that you consult with a professional experienced in all aspects of framing. Before that person can begin preparing your art, they will need to know if this is a piece you plan to keep forever, a very expensive piece or family heirloom, or something you like but aren't attached to for the long term. This will have a bearing on the handling of your piece.

Through the years, the most common types of framing for fine art have been termed "conservation," "archival" and "museum." In each case, different materials were chosen to come into direct contact with the artwork, affecting the long-term preservation in the mounting, matting and framing.

Today, the terms "archival" and "conservation" seem to be interchangeable. In fact, some professional framers say that all three terms now have essentially the same meaning. The consensus is that, for fine art, only 100% rag board and acid-free materials should be used in matting and framing. Nothing containing acids, pollutants, small pieces of metal, etc., should come into contact with your piece, contaminating it.

Common signs of damage from poor materials include yellow "burnt" edges on an unframed artwork and corrugation imprints in the back of a piece mounted on cardboard.

Matting and Framing

Certain general rules apply to framing. If artwork is permanently mounted on anything such as a piece of foamcore (which may not matter in the case of a poster or a piece that has lesser value), it is devaluated. When using mountboards, mats, interleaving, backing papers or any other element that will come into contact with your artwork, make sure it's 100% rag fiber, completely acid free. If you're matting artwork and storing it, be sure to use acid-free buffered tissue between the pieces of art you are stacking.

Lesser quality materials, regardless of their beauty, may contaminate your art and cause irreparable damage. When purchasing a piece already framed, make sure you know what materials were used in the process. Leave *nothing* to question.

Expertly matted and framed by a professional, your artwork should last many decades beyond you.

The Survival Guide to Buying Art

INSURING ART

Common sense is your best guide to protecting the safety of your artworks. Still, you can save yourself considerable money and concern by following these simple guidelines.

Document your art collection (all types of art) immediately upon acquisition using a notebook or forms available at your local bookstore. Provide information on each piece using the following list:

Artist's name

Item's name

Series' name

Year

Edition and number (if applicable)

Copy of Certificate of Authenticity (if applicable)

Size and dimensions

Date of purchase

Where purchased and cost

Any additional expenses (crating, shipping, insurance for shipping, etc.)

Any special markings (signed by the artist to you, etc.)

A history of the piece

The location of the artwork in your home (in case of fire, theft, damage)

Your insurance company

Insuring Art

Photographing your collectibles is a very effective safeguard. Several pieces may be grouped together as long as they are easy to identify in the photo. Many insurance companies will accept home videos in the place of photos, but ask your carrier for specific guidelines.

Make sure to inform your insurance company if you have a variety of artwork. Many policies group art into a single category, so it will be up to you to make sure your collection is scheduled properly.

If your art is *appreciating* in value, verify that your insurance company isn't *depreciating* the same piece. If the artist has brochures, magazine articles or other history materials, collect and keep them to be used as documentation in the case of resale or the filing of a claim.

INTERESTING LAWS THAT PERTAIN TO ART

The following California statutes are not generally known to the public. Although specific to California at this time, they are of vital importance and may become accepted nationwide in the near future.

(A) California Civic Code, Section 986, requires that when a fine art work (once it's sold) is resold by the owner for a price of more than one thousand dollars ($1000), that 5% of the "gross sales price" must be paid to the artist. If the seller cannot locate the artist, the royalty must be deposited with the California Arts Council, which is obligated to attempt to contact the work's creator. If it's unclaimed after seven years, the council may apply the money to its programs.

(B) Under California Penal Code Section 536a, a consignee (dealer or gallery) is obligated, upon written demand from the artist (consignor), to furnish the artist with the name and address of the purchaser of that artist's work as well as the price paid.

When a dealer or gallery sells a work of art that has been consigned to it by an artist, it's often important for the artist to ascertain the identity of the purchaser of that work. This information can facilitate arrangements for loans to future exhibitions, be used for biographical notations and scholarly listings, and assist the artist in enforcing certain legal rights under contract, copyright, resale-royalty and art-preservation laws.

GLOSSARY

Absorbent ground — A base (chalk) ground that is used to absorb liquid from the paint.

Acid-free — A neutral or slightly basic pH.

Acid-free board — Matboard that has a pH value of 7 or greater.

Acrylic resin paint — A synthetic oil-compatible medium thinned with turpentine and linseed oil. Quick drying.

Acetate ink — A special ink used on slippery surfaces.

Acetate (prepared or prefixed) — Clear, treated plastic used for overlay in photography, color separations and in graphic art. Also can be painted on without peeling or crawling.

After — In art, "after" identifies an etching, embossing, etc., deliberately copied from the original by another artist. Usually it's done in a different medium than the original.

Albumen print — A photographic-type print very common in the 19th century. Collodion wet-plate negatives were printed on paper coated with a salt and egg white solution. This would result in a yellow print that would then be toned to sepia.

Alpha or high-alpha — An alpha-cellulose which is free of acids. A high alpha content paper should have a near neutral pH.

Arches (D'Arches) — The trade name of a popular 100% rag watercolor paper from France. It comes in different textures as well as different weights.

Artist's Proof (A/P) — A proof outside the regular edition but from the same plates without changes. The artist usually reserves these prints for personal use or sale. Customarily, up to 10% of the total edition are A/P's.

Autolithography — The artist's drawing of an original work on the litho stone or plate.

Batik — The wax-resist art process used in textile design.

Benday — A printing process using screens of different dot patterns to mechanically produce effects of shading.

Bite — A term used in engraving, to bite (or etch) from a metal plate.

Blockprint — A relief process in which the image is printed utilizing the surface of block, made of wood, linoleum or another material. The recessed areas of the cut block will not print.

Bon A Tirer (B/A/T) — When the artist is satisfied with the final proof, this term indicates that the printer may proceed with finishing the edition. The print is marked Bon A Tirer (good to pull). There is only one B/A/T, and it usually goes to the printer.

Cancellation print — When the edition is completed, the plate, block, stone or whatever's used is defaced or destroyed to ensure no reprint. The one print made from the canceled plate is called the cancellation print.

Cellout — A print made with celluloid dissolved in acetone, applied to metal plates and printed in intaglio or relief.

Celluloid print — A print made from an image scratched into a sheet of celluloid in drypoint manner and printed in intaglio.

Cerography — Any type of painting on wax.

Chain and laid lines — This is the pattern of perpendicular lines visible in some handmade papers when you hold them up to the light. They are widely spaced and are crossed which is due to the wires used in the paper mold.

Chine Collé — A paper collage process in which sheets of paper are laminated together with the pressure of an etching press and glue. The printmaker can achieve color areas without using a separate plate and also use paper that otherwise would be too fragile for the printing process.

Chromolithography — The way of making multicolor lithographs by using different stones or plates for each color of ink.

Chop marks — A chop mark, or blind stamp, is a small inked or embossed seal impressed into the print by either the printer or the publisher. In the case of the printer, it means that he or she commissioned and published the edition of prints. Dealers and galleries may also have a chop mark indicating that they sold the print.

Cliché verre — An image drawn with an etching needle on the darkened surface of a glass plate, from which a photographic print is made.

Collector's marks — Collectors sometimes affix a mark or monogram on a print, either on the back or front.

Collage — The use of various materials adhered to a surface to create an image.

Collagraph — A collage of materials attached to the surface of a plate and printed in either intaglio or relief.

Collotype — A photomechanical process involving a plate coated with gelatin, often used for high-quality reproductions.

Colored print — A print produced in color using a separate plate for each color, by inking separate areas of the plate, by printing through stencils or by using inks of different thickness.

Color separation — Making a separate plate for each color to be printed.

Cotton — The fiber often used in fine art papers. Cotton linters, the fuzz of short fibers clinging to cotton seeds, are frequently used in papermaking. Cotton rags can make a high-quality paper.

Chroma — The concentration, intensity and saturation of color that identifies the chromatic colors from white and black.

Counterproof — An image made by transferring a wet proof to another sheet of paper. The design appears as it is on the original plate.

Dates — It's customary for the artist to put the date (sometimes month and year, or only year) on the print in pencil. This is the date the print was signed.

Debossment — Cutting below or pushing into the image surface.

Deckle — The irregular edge in handmade paper.

Dedicated print — The artist sometimes signs and dedicates a print to someone, some cause, organization, etc. These prints may be from the regular edition, artist proofs or extra prints of the edition. They're also called presentation prints.

Desensitize — A term used in lithography to describe areas on stone or plate rendered insensitive to grease with acidified gum etch.

Diptych — A picture (or print) painted on two panels, canvas, etc.

Documentation — Information on artwork telling the artist's name, printer's name, location of the studio, date and other valuable data.

Dotted print — A print made using a 15th century technique in which metal plates are engraved with a variety of goldsmith's punches. They were printed in relief, resulting in a white-line image.

Dry lithography — A lithographic printing technique using a chemical coating that repels ink.

Drypoint — An intaglio process in which lines are engraved directly into a plate with a hard steel or diamond point. When printed, the line has a "furry" quality.

Edition — The number of prints created from one work authorized for distribution.

Embossing — Printing by pressure to produce a raised, three-dimensional effect in the paper. Blind Embossing is done without ink.

Engraving — An intaglio process in which lines are engraved directly into a surface.

Etching — A process of exposing an engraved plate (or metal plate, glass, etc.) to acid. An acid-resistant substance is applied over the plate and then selectively removed. The areas exposed to the acid are etched.

Excudit — A notation that sometimes indicates reworking and reissue.

Exc., Excud — Short for the Latin word *excusit* meaning "has published it." When it follows a name on a print, it refers to the printer as differentiated from the one who engraved.

Format — The shape and size of a print, book or other printed material.

Frottage — See "rubbing."

Foxing — The appearance of brownish spots on old paper.

Fresco — The method of painting on moist lime plaster with water-based pigments.

Gesso — Gypsum (or plaster of Paris); when mixed with glue it's used as a surface coating.

Gouache — A technique using opaque pigments in a water base.

Grain — Surface texture of wood, paper.

Graphic — An original work of art on paper. In a broad sense, it's art represented by printing, drawing and painting.

Ground — In etching, this term refers to the type of acid-resistant covering applied to the plate. By coating the plate, the artist can draw with a stylus, which removes lines of the ground and exposes the plate to the acid.

Guide proof — When an artist employs a printer or workshop, he or she works with the printer to obtain a perfect print to use as as an example for the edition prints to follow. Many times the first print pulled fails to satisfy the artist. This is known as the "guide proof" and on it the artist notes any areas that must be improved. A perfect print is created. This print is then shown to the artist and, if approved, he or she signs it and marks it Bon A Tirer. The Bon A Tirer is then used as a guide by the printer to complete the edition.

Gum arabic — The binder used in watercolors, originating from the gum of the acacia tree.

Hashira-e — A long, narrow Japanese print designed to be hung on a pillar or column.

Heliogravure — Photomechanical intaglio process.

HMP — Symbol for handmade paper.

Hors Commerce (H/C) — Prints pulled with the edition prints and marked by the artist for business only. These prints are used for entering shows and art fairs, also for advertising or sales. Normally they're not sold.

Hot Pressed paper (HP) — A dense, smooth paper used for drawing and watercolor painting.

Hyalography — The method of engraving on glass with emery or a diamond-cutting tool. Also done with an etching solution.

Impression — Any print made from a plate, stone or block. Also the contact of paper and printing surface.

Impressist (Imp.) — In print, it's synonymous with "exc."

Ingres paper — Heavily textured paper. Comes in a variety of colors and is used frequently with pastels.

Ink — A pigment in liquid or paste form.

Intaglio — Any printmaking technique involving engraving or cutting below a plate surface. It's printed by rubbing ink into the cuts and then pulling the plate through a press under pressure, which forces ink into the paper.

Ivory board — Good for illustrations.

Japon paper — Made with an irregular and mottled surface. Often used for greeting cards.

Laid paper — Handmade paper showing the parallel grid pattern of a wire mold.

Letterpress — Relief printing.

Limited edition — A predetermined number of prints made from a master. The number of the edition is known and, after that number is reproduced, the plate is defaced to guarantee the edition.

Lithography — A printmaking process based on the incompatibility of oil and water. An image is drawn on stone or plate with ink and is chemically treated so the image attracts ink and the wet blank areas reject it. The printing surface is flat.

Mackle — A flaw caused by creasing of the paper during printing.

Maculature — The pulling of a second proof without reinking the plate. Normally a weaker image.

Makeready — Building up weak areas in relief printing by pasting more paper on the back of the block.

Margin — The space around the image area of a print.

Mat — A heavy paper that surrounds the art, enhancing its appearance, separating the art from glass and protecting.

Mezzotint — An intaglio process in which the plate surface is uniformly roughened with a tool called a rocker. When printed, the background is even and black. The artist may achieve gray to white tones by scraping and sanding the surface flatter, working dark to light.

Monoprint (Monotype) — A print made by applying ink or oil paint directly on a plate (glass, wood, etc.) and then transferring the image to a sheet of paper by rubbing or by using a press. This is for any print process that does not allow duplication.

Mordant — (a) The acid in which an etching plate is immersed. (b) Adhesive film used in applying gold leaf.

Mountboard — Stiff cardboard used for mounting artwork.

Museum board — Acid-free, pure rag mountboard.

Numbered and signed — On a limited edition, the artist signs and numbers each piece. For example, 75/150 would mean that you have the 75th piece of an edition totaling 150.

Offset lithography — A planographic process in which the image is transferred from a plate or stone to the rubber roller of a press and then to the paper (rather than directly from plate to paper).

Oleograph — An early period color lithograph printed in oil inks to look like an oil painting.

Original print — A print designed and printed by the artist, usually signed and numbered in a limited edition.

Paper — A flexible, thin sheet made from a pulp of rags, wood or other fibrous material.

Papercut — A print made from either cutout shapes in heavy paper or cardboard mounted on a plate, then varnished and inked in relief and/or intaglio.

Paper plate lithography — The technique of using a special paper plate that can be easily carried and used for sketching. It can be printed on a variety of presses.

Parchment — A writing material made by separating the inner side of a sheepskin from the woolen outer side. The skin is sized to make it suitable for writing. Parchment is not a paper.

Paste print — A print made from intaglio plates impressed into paper that has been covered with a pulplike substance.

Patina — The green rusty material that develops on bronze and other metals as they age.

pH — A chemical symbol that indicates the potential of hydrogen present in a substance. It's measured on an acidity-alkali scale with a range of 0-14. Paper is most stable at 7 to 8.5, having as little acidic content as possible and as little alkali as possible.

Photolithography — A lithographic process involving photographic transfer of an image to a sensitized litho stone or plate.

Photo-silkscreen — The transfer of photographic images to silkscreen.

Plein air — The French term indicating that a work has either been done or at least has the look of having been painted outside, "in the open air."

Planographic — Printed from a level surface, directly or by offset.

Plate mark — An indentation on paper left by the outside edges of a plate or stone.

Photomultiplier — A photoemissive photoelectric cell that amplifies emitted electrons and converts them into brighter light; an electric signal.

Pochoir — A process involving the application of color through stencils and used for reproducing works of art in small editions.

Polyautography — The early name for lithography.

Polyptych — Artwork with more than three sections.

Printer's proof — If the artist requests that the Bon A Tirer print be returned to him or her after the edition is printed, then custom allows the printer to retain one print for him or herself. This print is signed by the artist and marked Printer's Proof.

Progressive proof — During the development of a B/A/T and prior to printing an edition of multi-colored prints, a proof (known as the progressive proof) is made of each color or combination of colors to guide the printer in editing. The final combination of all colors in one print produces the B/A/T. Normally the progressive proofs are retained by the printer.

Proof — An impression taken of an artwork at any stage, such as artist proof or trail proof.

Publisher's proof — The same as hors commerce.

Pulp — The mixture of a macerated substance (cotton, rag, wood) in water that can be molded, pressed and dried to make paper.

Rag paper — Fine paper made of linen rags, free of wood pulp.

Register — A mark used as a guide for the correct placement of the paper when printing one color over another.

Relief etching — A technique in which acid-resistant varnish is applied to a metal plate so that the negative areas (background) are etched away and the image is left in relief.

Relief printing — In this method of printing, the image area is raised on a block or plate, either by cutting away the non-image area or by building up the level of the image. The image is inked and transferred under pressure to the paper.

Remarque proof — A proof print with the artist's notes and drawings indicating how he or she plans to proceed in the process.

Remarque — A popular technique in which the artist does a small original drawing on a limited-edition print.

Reproduction — An artwork copy, often in a different medium.

Restrike — A reprinting of a plate, usually unsigned and unnumbered.

Retirage — French for "pulling again." When used in graphics, it's the pulling of a second print without re-inking the plate.

Reverse — To flop the picture to change direction. In art, to change negative to positive or vice versa.

Reverse etching — Surface inking an intaglio plate, then printing it like a woodblock.

Rice paper — The pith of a plant found in Taiwan. It's lightweight paper made into different sizes, weights, colors and textures; used for watercolors, inks and printing.

Rubbing (Frottage) — A printlike impression made by rubbing ink on a sheet of paper placed over a raised or carved surface.

Sand-ground aquatint (Carborundum print) — A print made by pressing a sheet of sandpaper into an etching plate and running them through the press together.

Scratchboard (Scraperboard) — The artist covers a drawing surface with ink and then, on the dried ink, uses a sharp tool to make the design by scraping (or scratching) away the top layer of ink.

Serigraphy — Printing by the silkscreen process. The term generally applies to fine art rather than to commercial works. See Silkscreen.

Signature — (a) The artist's name on artwork. (b) In printing, the term refers to the grouping of pages according to the folding of the paper coming from the press. Usually the printing signatures consist of 16 or 32 pages.

Silkscreen — The printmaking process by which soft inks are squeezed through the open areas in silk mesh or similar material stretched on wooden frames, with the area to be left unpainted previously stopped out. A design is cut into a stencil which is on top of the screen or is painted on to the screen with a varnish or other liquid resist. Then ink or paint is wiped across the surface of the screen with a squeegee so it penetrates on the surface below, where the screen is not covered by the stencil. By making more than one screen for the design (and by using different colors), it builds a complex print. This technique was developed after the start of the 20th century.

Sizing — Gelatinous or glutinous substance used to fill the pores of paper or fabric.

Spatter — A technique in which tusche is spattered on litho stone to produce halftones.

Special edition — In Europe, it's the custom for the artist to mark his or her artist's proofs as "special edition." These are numbered in Roman numerals to differentiate them from the "edition." They are identical to the edition prints, but are for the artist's personal use and sale. In some cases the artist may rework a canceled plate to produce a different but similar print and publish a smaller special edition with the same name as the original edition but with the Roman numeral II after it. They may also be known as "preferred" or "reserved edition."

State proof — A stage in the development of a print. Proofs are pulled after significant changes have been made on the plate and show the progress of the print.

Stencil — A cutout used to define and control the application of ink or color to any surface.

Stripple print — A method of creating a print by using minute dots to build up a design. Stripple is used in etching and engraving and tends to resemble crayon.

Strippling — The watercolor painting technique when the design is composed of small dots or dabs of color.

Surface printing — A printmaking method where ink (or color) is applied directly to the plate, after which paper is laid on it and either daubed or rolled.

Three-dimensional — Indicating width, depth, and height.

Transfer — The method of moving an image from one surface to another.

Transfer lithograph — Design drawn by the artist with grease crayon or tusche on special paper and transferred to litho stone or zinc plate, eliminating reversal of the image.

Triptych — A set of three panels of a painting, print, etc.

Trucage — A fake or forgery.

Tusche — Fluid used to paint the design in silk screening and lithography.

Uninked intaglio — Blind embossing from an intaglio plate.

Value — The degree of darkness or lightness of a color against a scale from white to pure black. The darker and lighter colors are known as lower (black) and higher (white) value.

Varnish — A protective covering of natural or synthetic resin. This cover protects the paints surface.

Vellum — Originally a name for parchment, now used for Japanese and other fine, sized papers.

Viscosity — The rate of a liquids flow, a characteristic utilized in multicolor printing from one plate with various inks combined. Also the degree of denseness in ink or paint.

Viscosity printing — An etching method that allows multicolor printing from a single plate.

Vinyl inks — Used in silk screen for printing on vinyl.

Wash — Diluted tusche or ink used to produce halftones on litho stones or plates.

Watermark — A translucent design impressed with wire during the paper-making process.

Wax proofing — The technique of pulling a rough print from a paper covered in melted wax.

White line engraving — The design is carved into the surface, which consequently appears as a white design on a black field.

Window board — The piece of matboard in which an opening is cut to allow the display of the artwork.

Woodcut — A relief print made by cutting into the side grain of a wood block with sharp tools and printed from resulting raised areas.

Wood-pulp paper — Paper made of cellulose wood tissue bleached with sulfurous acids. Not generally used for print collectors.

Wove paper — Paper made on a fine wire-mesh screen in a mold.

Zincography — An old term for lithography on zinc plates.